THE
Archive Photographs
SERIES

REDDITCH

Detailed Particulars

of a

VALUABLE FREEHOLD CINEMA

AND VARIETY THEATRE

known as

"The Picture House,"

REDDITCH

(BIRMINGHAM 13 MILES. LONDON 108 MILES.)

To be offered for Sale by Auction, as a Going Concern,

At the GRAND HOTEL, COLMORE ROW, BIRMINGHAM

On Wednesday, the 24th day of November, 1926

at SIX o'clock in the Evening (subject to Conditions then to be produced).

SOLICITORS:

Messrs. BROWNING & CO.,
Evesham Chambers,
Evesham Street, REDDITCH

AUCTIONEERS:

Messrs. Leonard Carver & Co.
39-40, Bennett's Hill, BIRMINGHAM
Telephone: Central 461-462. AND LONDON

in conjunction with

Mr. THOMAS F. HEMMING,
6, Bates Hill, REDDITCH. Telephone 92.

Sales particulars from a 1926 brochure advertising the sale by auction of The Picture House later to become known as The Select, The Regal and The Flea Pit.

THE
Archive Photographs
SERIES

REDDITCH

Compiled by
Phillip Coventry

First published 1997

The Chalford Publishing Company
St Mary's Mill, Chalford,
Stroud, Gloucestershire, GL6 8NX

ISBN 0 7524 0735 X

Typesetting and origination by
The Chalford Publishing Company
Printed in Great Britain by
Redwood Books, Trowbridge

Contents

Acknowledgements		6
Introduction		7
1.	Town Centre	9
2.	Side Streets	29
3.	Events and Happenings	49
4.	General Life	65
5.	Around and About	85
6.	Military and Martial	101
7.	Needles, Springs and Bikes	111

Acknowledgements

Much of this book is made up from photographs and postcards from my own collection. However, I would like to take this opportunity to say thank you to the following people, for the encouragement, support, information and loan of material so freely given:

Mike Wojczynski, Roger Vale, Philip Jarvis, Colin Clough, Malcolm Barrett, Pam Draycott, Norman Turner, June Victory, Alan White, Kathleen Carr, Norman Neasom, David Morgan, Irene Yates, John Smith, Sheila Young, Anne Bradford and John Maries. A special thankyou is due to Melvyn Amos, a fellow collector, whose generosity in the unquestioning loan of his own material knew no bounds.

Special thanks are reserved also for my friend Alan Foxall for the unflinching loan of material he may otherwise have used elsewhere and for the considerable support and assistance he has unselfishly given and which has made the production of this book an easier project than it might otherwise have been.

Thanks also to my wife Pamela for the unstinting hours spent at the keyboard turning my 'demented scrawl' into wonderfully legible type.

If I have left anyone out whom I should have thanked I humbly offer my sincere apologies.

Last but in no way least I would like to express some sympathy for, and pay tribute to, my family who for many years have stoically contended with the obsessions of a fanatical collector.

Phillip J. Coventry

Introduction

Until I was approached by the publishers I had not given a moment's thought to appearing in print. However, the enquiry came from Chalford Publishing last year, and the more I thought about it the more the idea started to appeal.

There is no doubt that the thought of having your name on the cover of any book is uplifting, but if that book is one that deals with a topic that has become a passion, consuming all available free time, then the pleasure is so much the greater. This book, then, is the ideal opportunity to indulge myself and at the same time to share with everyone else my interest in 'Old Redditch'. The selection of photographs and ephemera has largely been made from my own collection of views and scenes around the town and surrounding area.

I've tried to cover as large an area and as wide a range of subjects as possible within the scope of the material available. If the reader gets only a fraction of the pleasure from looking at the images in this book that I have had from collecting and compiling the contents, then my time will not have been wasted.

This book is dedicated to
the memory of
Audrey Evelyn Winifred Coventry
1921-1990

One
Town Centre

In the centre of this group pictured in Church Green East around 1905 is 'Little Fanny', a dwarf who lived in Peakman Street.

Now the Church Green East branch of Lloyds Bank, at the time of this postcard, c. 1910, this was the Capital and Counties Bank. Here the staff take a well-earned break to pose for the camera. The imposing portico was later moved to its present position nearer the right-hand corner of the building.

The west side of Market Place around 1905. Prominently featured is the shop of Mr A. Bell who was for many years the agent in the town for Royal Enfield Bicycles.

The promenade on an autumn day around 1910. In the background behind the group of people can be seen the old cottage which was demolished to make way for the Redditch Building Society offices.

This charming postcard from around 1910 shows how far the fashion in prams has moved on in the last eighty years. It also gives some idea of how quiet the roads were.

Evesham Street, *c.* 1915, looking north towards the church. The photograph was taken by Mr Albert Green. Mr Green was employed in the fishing-tackle trade for many years and was also a keen amateur photographer. Eventually, he turned professional and opened premises in Grove Street.

Church Green, *c.* 1910. Prominently featured is Lewis Bros.' shop. Lewis Bros. were among the first photographers to establish a studio in Redditch and were responsible for recording many of the important events in the area.

Unicorn Hill around 1930. The message on the back of this postcard reads: 'Redditch – where the needles come from'.

Smallwood Hospital was paid for by the brothers William and Edwin Smallwood, two local needlemakers. The hospital was opened in 1895. The land and buildings cost around £15,000.

Ispley Green around the turn of the century. The Baptist chapel in the background was knocked down to provide building land for Herbert Terry's factory and offices. The oak tree was planted to commemorate Queen Victoria's Golden Jubilee in 1887. This area was formerly known as Pool Place and once contained the notorious Big Pool, reputed to be the source of the 1832 cholera outbreak.

Alcester Street on a busy day around 1907. The signwriting on the gable end of Watkins' tea rooms is still visible today. There are no horses in view in the picture but you can see where they have been!

St Stephen's church. Due to the poor quality of the stone used to build St Stephen's, the fabric of the building seems to need constant repair. This photograph was taken in the summer of 1906 when scaffolding was erected around the spire.

Alcester Street in the 1940s. Richmond's fish shop can be clearly seen as can Murdochs, the gents' outfitters and Hedges, chemist. In the background are the Nags Head and the Rising Sun.

The window of Curry's shop in Market Place soon after it opened around 1934. Before they became a major electrical retailer, Curry's also sold bicycles. The author purchased his first bike from Curry's in Market Place around 1955.

A 1940s view of Evesham Street. Note the hand-cart for delivering milk, and The Motor House garage with the petrol pumps passing over the pavement.

Evesham Street, *c.* 1910. The corner site occupied by Liptons was later taken up by Hopkins the jewellers. The Vine Inn was demolished in 1926 and rebuilt as The Talbot.

No collection of Redditch scenes and views would be complete without one of the church gardens showing the fountain, bandstand and church. The fountain was built in 1883, the original bandstand in 1898 and the church in 1855.

Evesham Street in Edwardian times. This postcard was published by Mrs A. Scriven who ran a stationers in Evesham Street.

Evesham Street looking north around 1910. The second shop along on the right is Clarke's, the photographer, where this postcard was produced.

The parade looking towards Smallwood Hospital from a photograph taken by L. Sealey around 1910.

Evesham Street around 1910. Spencer's radio shop is in the foreground. The Fleece Inn with its magnificent hanging lamps is in the centre of the picture.

Church Green East around 1905. A prominent feature is the horse's head displayed above the shop of Oliver Free the saddler.

Evesham Street, *c.* 1905. The shop on the right-hand corner is Cranmore Simmons, a general furniture dealer. James Huins' shoe emporium is on the left-hand corner.

The Parade in 1905. This photograph was taken from outside the library and institute at the top of Church Road.

The Parade around 1925. This photograph was taken from the top of Market Place and shows the war memorial which was erected after the First World War.

Redditch police station in the 1950s. The police station was located in Church Road alongside the Magistrates' Court. The building just in view on the right-hand side was the labour exchange.

The Co-op shop which stood for many years on the corner of Evesham Street and George Street. The Co-op was a major retailing force in Redditch, dealing in everything from milk to furniture.

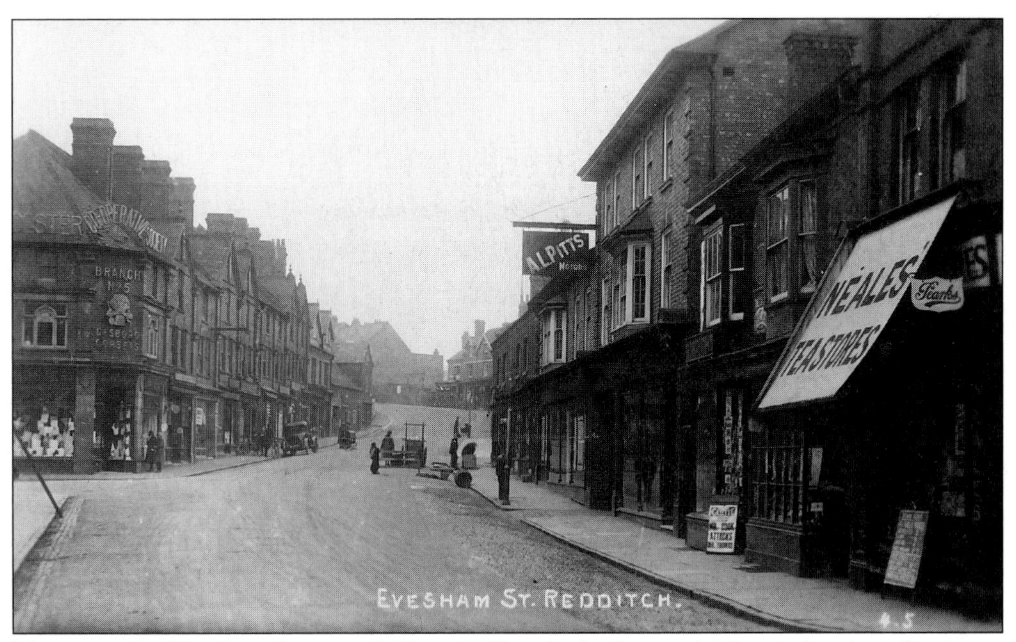

The top end of Evesham Street with Front Hill in the background. The workmen in the centre appear to be laying slabs.

A view from the bottom of Front Hill with Evesham Street in the background and Park Road centre left. The large building in the left foreground was the Council Offices when this photograph was taken around 1910.

Robert Ladbury's shop in Evesham Street around 1910. This stood on the east side of the street and was later demolished to make way for the block known as Commercial Buildings which eventually became Humphries' shoe shop.

The Parade on a market day around 1905. Stockbridge's drapers shop and Dale Fortie's piano store can be seen in the background.

The White Swan on the corner of Vine Street and Evesham Street (Vine Street later became Worcester Road). The proprietor at the time was David Hemming who held the licence between 1903 and 1910.

Another fine view of Evesham Street featuring Clarke's shop, purveyors of postcards and photographs including this one. This scene probably dates from the 1920s.

Red Lion Street in the 1960s. Next to the fire station is the former scouring mill of the Brabrant Needle Company which became Maxwell Jones' studio. The three-storey house in the centre of the picture is No. 24, the birthplace and home for twenty-five years of the author of this book.

The top end of George Street in the 1960s taken from the rear entrance of the bus station looking towards Johnson's shop with the houses of Ipsley Street peeping over the top of the wall around the youth club.

Alcester Street in the 1960s showing the Nags Head and The Rising Sun. In between lies Smith Street, which contained one of the last two working blacksmith shops in the town.

The corner of Red Lion Street and Ipsley Street in the 1960s showing the start of the row of one-up one-down cottages that lay below the level of the road. The white building on the corner was 'Chippy' Lee's chip shop.

The impact of the new town redevelopment is evident here. On the left is the side of the fire station. The waste ground in the foreground in front of Heartbeat springs factory is what was The Brabrant needle factory and Nos 24 and 26 Red Lion Street. This scene was captured in the late 1960s.

More ravages of development. The Heartbeat factory is almost gone and the Palace Theatre looms over the top of what is left of Alcester Street. This picture is from the late 1960s.

Two

Side Streets

Prospect Hill looking towards Albert Street and British Mills around 1910. Note how the cart is parked at an angle to stop it rolling back down the hill. The Scourers Arms is believed to be in the background.

Prospect Hill from the top looking down around 1905. On the right is Clarke's factory. The three-storey house on the left once belonged to Richard Hemming, the needlemaker, and beside it is the notorious Hemmings Entry.

Worcester Road, looking towards Park Road around 1905. The photograph was taken by H.A. Clarke, the Redditch photographer. The card was written by someone who lived at 'Eversleigh', a house on Worcester Road.

St Stephen's Church Institute taken soon after it opened in 1910. In the 1950s the Institute was used by St Stephen's School as an overspill. This was where the author of this book sat his eleven plus exams in 1955.

Oakley Road in the 1920s with the spire of St Stephen's peeping over the rooftops.

Oakley Road just above its junction with Park Road around 1910. Oakley Road is one of the many roads in the area with a connection with the Windsors of Hewell. As well as owning much of the land on which Redditch streets were laid out, the family also owned an estate called Oakley Park in Shropshire.

Mount Pleasant looking north with The Plough and Harrow in the background, *c.* 1910. The trees growing through the pavements here have long since gone.

A view of Millsboro Road composed around 1910 by Mr Albert Green, the photographer from Grove Street. The row of three-storey houses on the right was demolished to make way for Terry's factory.

Bromsgrove Road looking towards the town around 1905, with the Queens Head on the right-hand side. At the time the licensee would have been Mr R. Edwards.

Some photographers used a cut-out device to make their postcards more interesting. This example of Mount Pleasant dates from around 1914.

Hewell Road, *c.* 1905. This postcard was written and sent to Smethwick by Blanche, who lived in the third house on the right.

The top of Holloway Lane, *c.* 1910, with the tower of Mount Carmel church glimpsed in the background. The customary group of children are on hand to pose for the photographer, including a group of scouts.

Headless Cross in the 1920s. In the background is the White Hart while on the right-hand side is The Bell, whose licensee at the time would have been either James Wood or A. Locke.

Evesham Road, Crabbs Cross around 1905. A scene not so very different now with the exception of the traffic. Try parking or crossing the road today!

Studley Road in the 1940s before Lodge Farm School was built. The houses on the right were erected by Mr Bert Batty in the 1930s.

Rectory Road around 1915 before pavements were put in to serve the houses on the right-hand side.

Ivor Road looking towards the golf course, in the early 1930s. One of the steepest hills in Redditch, Ivor Road was, and still is, a gruelling test for cyclists, not to mention some older motors.

Beoley Brook around 1910, before the road was taken over the river. This was once the main route from Redditch into Birmingham and was very dangerous when the river was in full flow.

Ipsley Court, c. 1905. This was once the home of Walter Savage Landor, the poet. In the background is Ipsley church.

Ipsley Rectory; the façade is much more recent than the rest of the building which is medieval in origin.

Salop Road with the cemetery in the background. This is another of the roads in the area whose name has associations with the Windsors of Hewell.

Foxlydiate post office, probably around 1915. It is believed that the two girls posing for the camera are the daughters of Benjamin Lee, the postmaster.

Foxlydiate was a well-known beauty spot in the area and remained unchanged for many years. In 1903, however, it was the scene of a savage murder. This photograph was taken in the 1930s.

Mount Carmel church, Beoley Road around 1905. The church was built in 1834. It was one of the first significant Catholic churches to be built in the area after the Reformation in the sixteenth century.

'The Cedars'. This was once the imposing home near Hewell Road of Samuel Allcock, the fishing-tackle manufacturer.

St George's Road around 1910. The view is of the top half of the road looking towards Grove Street.

Birchfield Road when the roadway was narrower, the pavements wider and it was possible to walk across the road with safety.

Edward Street around 1905. Edward Street and Britten Street were two streets that joined Bromsgrove Road and Bridge Street and ran parallel to each other.

Oakley Road around the turn of the century. The view is of the top end of the road with the corner of Ludlow Road in the background.

Bates Hill around 1910, with the imposing structure of the Methodist church towering over everything. The church was demolished to make way for an electrical superstore.

The bottom half of St George's Road looking towards St George's church. The photograph was taken around 1910 from the point where Other Road crossed St George's Road.

Hewell Road around 1910. The raised pavement was a feature made necessary by the degree of slope of the surrounding land. Part of the pavement still exists today.

The junction of Beoley Road and The Holloway surmounted by the Kings Arms around 1915. Mount Carmel church is in the background.

Lodge Road looking towards the Warwick Arms around 1905. The usual band of children are on hand to pose for the photographer.

Mount Pleasant around 1907. The view is looking towards the town from just above the Crescent Works which can be seen in the background.

Mount Pleasant around 1905 looking south towards Headless Cross. The shops on the left are still trading today, but with different owners, of course!

The bottom end of Ipsley Street, *c.* 1910. This area was once known as Bredon. The Kings Arms is in the centre with the Wagon and Horses, now closed, in the background. Also in view is the Catholic church and the top of The Holloway.

Mount Pleasant, looking north around 1910. The shop on the right became the post office and is still trading. The author lived for a time at the prominently gabled house, the third from the left.

A fine view of the Plough and Harrow with a baker's cart making its rounds and Mount Pleasant Methodist Free Church, which was built in 1900, standing to the left. This photograph was taken around 1905.

Three

Events and Happenings

This early postcard is thought to show Hills Yard off Prospect Hill. In the background is a horse-drawn cart belonging to A. Smith the Redditch haulier.

In September 1913 an air-race took place between the aviators, B.C. Hucks (the first man to 'loop the loop') and Gustav Hamel. The race set off from Edgbaston and flew a 75-mile course around the Midlands, landing back at Edgbaston. With stops, the race took almost four hours. The Recreation Ground at Redditch was the first stopping place in the race.

The race was sponsored by the *Birmingham Daily Post* who reported that 30,000 spectators turned up to watch the event at Birmingham, including the Countess of Limerick, Lady Coventry and Neville Chamberlain. Gustav Hamel was the overall winner, beating Hucks by 20 seconds.

In 1920 a fund was started in Redditch to provide cots. Here, Mrs A. Terry starts the copper trail, aiming to collect a mile of pennies for the fund.

Alcester Street in 1907. Everyone is heading for a picnic. In the background are the cottages pulled down to build the Palace Theatre. On the corner of Grove Street is the shop of Millwards, the painter. The prominent signwriting remained for a long time afterwards.

The Band of Hope was formed in Redditch in 1854 because of the problems caused by a growing number of children roaming the streets with nothing to do. On this postcard from 1908, the Band is marching down Evesham Street.

Redditch market in the Market Place, *c.* 1910. It was common for the market to continue late into the night until all of the produce had been sold.

Market day in 1905. The market lasted well into the evening, the tradespeople only packing up when there was no chance of any more business and the customers hanging on till the last minute for final bargains.

Redditch Gymkhana, held at the sports ground in Red Lane, June 1906. The event was an annual affair to raise funds for worthy causes.

Redditch Fair 1906. The stall in the background belongs to C.S. Stockton, 'dealer in all types of foreign fruits.'

Redditch's version of the political arena when in July 1907, G. Roberts MP for Norwich and Peter Carram MP for Jarrow, addressed a meeting at the Recreation Ground on Easemore Road.

A Labour procession marching through the streets of Redditch, with banners flying and the band playing, heading to a public meeting at the Recreation Ground on Easemore Road around 1905.

The Temperance Society was a major force in Redditch around the turn of the century. The Temperance Hall was opened in 1885. Festivals and marches became an annual event. This postcard shows a march down Evesham Street in 1908.

The Band of Hope marching along Church Green East in 1908. In the background is the shop of Joseph Andrews, plumber and gas fitter.

The year is still 1908 and the same Band of Hope procession makes its way around Church Green East. The bearded gentleman in the first carriage is believed to be Herbert Terry, the founder of Terry's Springs.

Church parade in June 1910; the procession passing Webb's Bakery on the corner of Peakman Street and making its way towards Alcester Street.

The Temperance festival marching down Front Hill in 1907. Ladbury's Auction Rooms in the background are taking advantage of the crowds to advertise a forthcoming china auction.

Tom Clarke's Fair in June 1908 at Redditch. Notice how the crowd have all stopped to pose for the photographer.

Webheath Flower Show in 1907. A race is in progress and the crowd has congregated around the finishing line.

An ox-roast at the Red Lion, Hunt End in 1909. William Chambers was the licensee at the time.

A cyclists' meeting in Redditch in 1906. The single-storey shop in the background is Ladbury's, the greengrocers. Behind that is the tower of Townsend's Brewery.

The Band of Hope march passes from Church Green East into Alcester Street in May 1913.

Redditch Fair in 1906. The main feature is the switchback ride of Tom Clarke which would have been driven by a traction-engine.

Redditch Fair in 1907 with Chipperfield's Living Picture Show in the background doing very good business.

The 1907 Labour Demonstration. The procession is in full flow moving down Evesham Street toward the recreation ground in Easemore Road for some speechifying.

Another view of Redditch Fair in 1907 with Frank Winter's gingerbread stall in the foreground and the helter-skelter well featured on the left.

Coronation Day in 1911 when Redditch folk celebrated the coronation of King George V. This view was taken from The Parade with the band and the bandstand in the background.

Another scene from Coronation Day in 1911. The procession celebrating George V's coronation is making its way along Church Green East.

A Temperance festival march is forming, complete with portable lighthouse, at the top of William Street around 1910. St Stephen's church is just visible in the background.

PALACE THEATRE

Tel. 48 **REDDITCH** Tel. 48

Week commencing FEBRUARY 22nd

Box Office open 10.30 a.m. to 1 p.m. and 5 to 10 p.m. Times of Performances:

Monday to Friday, Once Nightly, 7.15. Saturday, Twice Nightly, 6.15 & 8.30

Prices: 3/6, 2/6, 1/6.

Special Children's **MIDGET TOWN MATINEE** *on Saturday*

at 2.30. Children half-price to all parts.

ALAN GALE

Presents

Star Cast of the Smallest

People in the World

MIDGET TOWN

ROYAL BRITISH LILLIPUTIANS DIRECT FROM U.S.A.

including

LEONARD : SEMON : SONIA

Miniature Magic Makers

TINY HETTY

Pocket Comedienne

WEE MARY BEST

3ft. Colotura Soprano

THE MAYOR OF MIDGET TOWN **MEET THE TINY MAYORESS**

SONNY (PETER PAN) RILEY

Direct from the Walt Disney film

TINY LITTLER

Smallest Man in the World

See the World's Smallest Choir. **These Midgets have to be seen to be believed.**

LA POUPEE

3ft. 6in. AERIALISTE. A Doll in the air flirting with death.

Introduced and compered by ALAN GALE

To avoid Disappointment BOOK NOW

A handbill for a show at the Palace Theatre, probably from the late 1940s. The Palace was originally built as a theatre, before becoming, amongst other things, a cinema, a dance hall, and a roller skating rink. It was restored into a theatre again during the new town development.

Four

General Life

Redditch Wednesday football team, 1908/9 season. Presumably, the team was made up of local shopkeepers since Wednesday in Redditch was half-day closing.

The Physical Culture Club met at the Drill Hall in Church Road to practise the 'black arts' of club swinging, weight-lifting, wrestling and other healthy pursuits.

Sunday school seniors posing for a group photograph. Fitz Heaphy is in the middle row, second from the left. Jack Baker (the butcher) is third from the left.

1st Redditch (St Stephen's) Guides. The leader, centre left, was the 'nit lady' who visited the local schools to check heads for unwelcome visitors.

The pupils and staff of Miss Heaphy's school, 1926. The school was off Evesham Street. The photograph was taken in the school gardens. Miss Heaphy is the lady in the centre.

Studley Castle was opened as an agricultural college for women in 1903 under the auspices of the Countess of Warwick. Here the pupils are staging an entertainment for the assembled audience using the temple in the grounds as a backdrop.

The Grove Inn was located just off the bottom of Crooks Lane in Studley. In 1910 there were enough regulars to make up a football team.

Smallwood Hospital and Police Orphanage Charity Cup final. It is a bleak February day for the match and there seem to be more players than spectators – not too different from some of today's matches!

The winter of 1907 must have been particularly hard as Lodge Pool froze over, as this picture of skaters on the pool can verify.

Redditch Rovers Second Reserves in 1910.

A family wedding group snapped by Joe Harman. The groom is thought to be Mr Rattue who was related to the station-master at Redditch.

Another family wedding group pictured by Joe Harman. This time one family involved is the Crumps. The groom is Harry Miles.

Redditch Town Band turned out for this function around 1900. The line up from left to right, back row: C. Guise, J. Perkins, F. Styler, S. Spencer. Middle row: H. Howes, C. Markham, J. Pulley, H. Lawrence, A. Spencer. Front row: G. Spencer, H. Sealey, S. Prescott, F. Shakespeare, W. Banner, F. Dyer, G. Bartlam, P. Spencer, C. Spencer. In front, kneeling: G. Lee and P. Phillips.

Redditch Hockey Club team, 1907. Among those pictured are: Revd Bradley, Messrs Styler, Leach, Shrimpton, Whitmore, Hill, Perkins, Lane, Thomas, Evans and Hill.

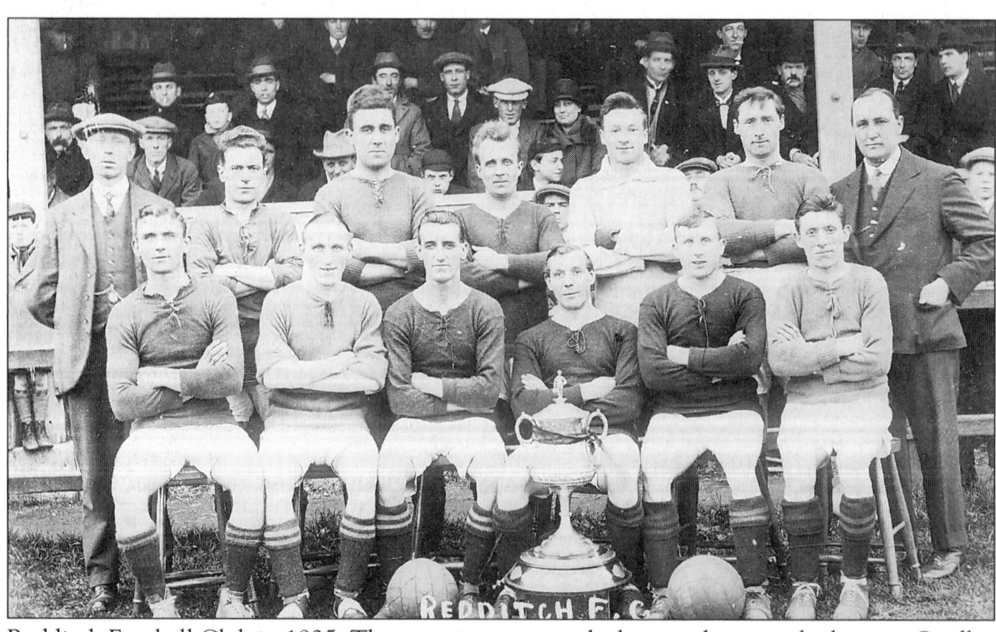

Redditch Football Club in 1925. The team is posing with the cup they won by beating Cradley in the final by 1-0. P. Bournville scored the winning goal.

The meet at Foxlydiate in 1906. Attitudes were different then – it is unlikely that any hunt saboteurs attended the scene.

Holyoaksfield Methodist Mission in Elm Road was the setting for this group photograph in the 1930s. Kenneth Bayliss is in the centre of the back row. Poole's factory can be glimpsed in the background.

In 1906 the NSPCC fête was held in the grounds of Foxlydiate House. The bearded man in the white hat is Canon Newton, his daughter is facing him holding a cup of tea.

Holmwood, which was built for Canon Horace Newton as his private residence in the 1890s. Subsequently, it was used as a children's recovery hospital, by the 'buffs' as a convalescent home and also by the development corporation as their headquarters. It has now been converted back to private residences.

The Earl of Plymouth officiates at the opening ceremony of Holmwood as a convalescent home in 1923.

The matron and staff posing on the steps of Holmwood soon after it opened as an RAOB convalescent home in 1923. The picture was taken by local photographer, John Hensman.

A view of Bentley Manor, the home of Mrs Cheape, known as the Squire of Bentley. This postcard was written by Mrs Cheape and posted to her son, Hugh Grey Cheape in Scotland in 1909.

Bentley Manor was the home of the Bentley Harriers, bred for hunting by Mrs Cheape, who can be seen in the centre. The black armband she wears is probably a sign of mourning for her daughter, Daisy, who was drowned in a boating accident in Scotland in 1896.

A set of postcards was produced to commemorate the opening of 'Holmwood' as an RAOB convalescent home in 1923. This card from the series shows the interior of one of the reception rooms.

Another interior view of Holmwood with gentlemen of a certain age, perhaps resting after lunch. The gentleman in the centre with the moustache also appears on the steps with the matron in an earlier view.

November 1919 and following the death of Mrs Cheape, her coffin leaves Bentley Manor for Bromsgrove station for the final journey to Wales, where she was buried.

Bentley smithy probably as it appeared around 1915. This postcard was produced by E.A. Hodges and posted in Redditch in 1917.

A very rare photograph of the Windsor Portrait Gallery of A.H. Clarke. The studio was to the rear of Clarke's shop in Evesham Street and is almost certainly where this postcard was produced.

St Stephen's was the first public school in Redditch. It was built around 1845 at the same time as the headmaster's house was built at the side of the school. This early photograph by J. Peakman probably dates from around 1880 and shows the headmaster with his family and staff and some of the older pupils.

Park Farm, Studley Road in 1912. On the top of the stack is A.W. Vale Senior, below him with the pitchfork is A.W. Vale Junior. Kate and Maud Vale are watching.

Britannia Batteries fire brigade and works police posing for the camera in the 1930s. The fire brigade, in the brass helmets, consisted of George Wright, George Campion, Jack Prentice, Jim Cull, Charles Kirby, Harold Sealey, Mr Browning, Herbert Perks, Fred Wedgbury and Charles Kibler.

This brass plate was dug up from a tip in Swindon. It was the label on a clothes washer patented by William Brewster of Redditch in 1867. The washer consisted of an iron kettle with a perforated base which allowed boiling water to circulate through the washing to force out the dirt.

Redditch fire brigade posing with their appliance 'the Baron'. The station was in Park Road before it moved to Red Lion Street and then, following redevelopment, to its present location on the Birmingham Road.

A charabanc belonging to Hills of Redditch, probably photographed in Easemore Road by Joe Harman in the 1930s.

The staff and station-master at Redditch station, c. 1905.

Repair work underway on the three-arch bridge over Windsor Road in 1908. In the background is Redditch Gas Works.

Studley and Astwood Bank station around 1910, before the days of Dr Beeching.

Redditch station looking north around 1905. A train is just arriving and the station is very crowded; perhaps a holiday excursion is about to depart.

A charabanc belonging to Regent Motorways who, for many years, operated from premises in Alcester Street, opposite the Palace Theatre.

Five

Around and About

Festivities underway at the Baptist treat at Doe Bank House, Astwood Bank, 1908.

Astwood Bank Adult Schools Sports Day, 1908. The procession winds its way through the village to the sports field. The adult school was formed to help with the educational needs of older people.

Astwood Bank cricket team around 1912. From left to right, back row: J. Days, B. Days, E. Paice, A. Days, W. Cooper, G.C. King, J.C. Hill. Front row: E. Parker (bowler hat), A. Wheeler, H. Wheeler (sitting), A. Perkins, H. Beard, F. Hill and A.H. Bayliss.

St Matthias and St George church choir in 1928. From left to right, back row: Reg Street, Vic Thomas, Harold Laight, Leslie Croxall, Robert Walton, Harold Grey, Michael Warwood, Bill Pratt, Bill Bennet. Middle row: Dorothy Sumners, Norah Lawrence, Rose Smith, Irene Ladbury, Winnie Cook, Revd Fred Brighton, Florence Croft, Mildred Bate, Phyllis Biddle, Margaret Croft, Ezme Houghton, Renee Houghton. Front row: Hubert James, George Walton, Ken Biddle, David Ratley, Harry James.

Astwood Bank with the bank and post office featured in the centre of the photograph. Although the traffic has greatly changed, the rest of the view is easily comparable with how it appears today.

Castle Street, Astwood Bank, *c.* 1906. It would seem that whenever a photographer appeared a group of children would materialise by magic to pose for the camera.

A grand photograph taken in Church Road outside the church, around 1910. Many of the children are carrying posies of flowers, probably for an event at church. Most of the children are in their Sunday best but one or two seem a little the worse for wear.

Cookhill Sunday school, *c.* 1908.

The Temperance Festival fête in 1907 moving off from Church Road, with the bands playing in the background and plenty of volunteers to carry the banner.

The procession is formed up in Church Road for the 1907 church treat. St Matthias and St George's church is in the background.

The Wesleyan Sunday school treat around the turn of the century. It was the fashion of the day to wear a hat – with only three exceptions, everyone in the photograph has their head covered.

The year is 1910 and the Temperance Festival is on the march again. This year fancy dress is the order of the day and national costumes seem to predominate.

Astwood Bank church treat, 1908. The procession has assembled outside the church in Church Road and is making its way through the village before ending up at the recreational ground.

'Dinnertime' reads the caption on this 1911 postcard of Perkins factory in Astwood Bank. In which case, the photographer was taking a risk in impeding the hungry workers!

The ceremony to lay the foundation stone for the Wesleyan School in Astwood Bank in 1907.

Astwood Bank, 1909. The Temperance Festival procession is making its way along Church Road accompanied by the regimental band.

Studley Picnic, 1906. It would seem that the entire population of the village has turned out. Fortunately, the local constabulary is on hand to control the crowds.

John Hill's butcher's shop, probably decorated for the Christmas festivities around 1905. Amongst the goods on display are sides of beef, whole pigs, sheep, turkeys, chickens, ducks and geese.

Studley Baptist fête, probably in the 1930s.

Sambourne Hall decorated for an event or celebration, possibly the 1937 coronation of George VI.

Built in 1834, Studley Castle was taken over around the turn of the century by the Countess of Warwick who turned it into an agricultural college for women.

A group of ladies from the agricultural college receiving a lesson in pruning.

The garden at the college with lots of busy fingers tying up plants.

Tending the bees at the apiary. The college sold off its surplus honey and other produce.

Hewell Grange came into the possession of the Windsor family in 1542. The Old Hall was built in 1711. It eventually fell into disrepair and was replaced around 1890 by the present structure which is now part of the remand centre complex.

The Lickey Monument was erected in memory of Other Archer, the 6th Earl of Plymouth, who died in 1833. The monument was raised by the Worcestershire Yeomanry Regiment he had led.

In the background is St Bartholomew's church, built in 1777 for the Earls of Plymouth when Redditch was still in the parish of Tardebigge. In the foreground is a stretch of the Birmingham–Worcester canal which was finally completed around 1815.

Tardebigge new wharf, *c.* 1920. In the centre is the Tunnel Tug *Worcester*. The canal reached the new wharf around 1813.

Tardebigge Church, once the parish church for Redditch until the chapel on the green was in place. The church was built in 1777 by the architect Francis Hiorn on instructions from the Earl of Plymouth.

Tardebigge School, *c.* 1910. From left to right: H. Gwynne, Ethel Cotterill, Mr Barraclough (the curate), Mrs Badger (Standard 3 teacher), Mrs Wurgin. Front row: Miss Garnham, Canon Dickens, Mr Dilkes (Head Teacher), Mrs Dilkes. Canon Dickens, the long-serving vicar of Tardebigge, took morning assembly at the school every morning.

Six

Military and Martial

Redditch Artillery saw service in the First World War. Here they are seen marching from their Easemore Road HQ to the railway station for the first leg of their journey.

Patriotism was the order of the day as this demonstration in Priory Square, Studley in 1915 shows. The town band is there; so too is the fire brigade, resplendent in their brass helmets.

In 1906, at the invitation of the Earl of Plymouth, the Worcestershire Yeomanry held a camp at Hewell Grange. Here we see the regimental band tuning up, probably for Sunday Parade.

Another view of the 1906 camp at Hewell Grange. This time the volunteers are marching to a church service. Note the bibles and hymn books some are carrying.

More recruits, this time marching through Priory Square, Studley in 1914, led by the Studley town band.

During the First World War The Tardebigge was put into use as a recovery hospital to allow wounded soldiers to convalesce. Here we see one of the wards laid out for a meal. Note the bedridden patients and nurses in the background.

The nursing and auxiliary staff take a break to pose for the camera, wielded by Mr Terry of Redditch. This scene is in the gardens to the rear of the hospital.

114 BOSCO'S BUDGET. 13th Nov. 1916

THEY'RE DOING THEIR "BIT."

GEO. JONES.
Late Washford Mills.

H. JONES.
Late Huins & Seden.

J. JONES.
Late Studley Castle.

O. JONES. (late B.S.A.)

MORRIS BRAY.
Late Crescent Works.

ALBERT COOPER.
Late Council House, B'ham.

A. JONES. (late Milward's).

All the above are members of one family. There are two other brothers, but as they are in France, we are unable to get photographs of them to complete the family.

A page copied from *Bosco's Weekly* published during the First World War, which shows one family's patriotic efforts.

The artillery volunteers about to embark on the train at Redditch station at the start of their service in the First World War.

In 1882 Major Corbett of the Worcestershire Yeomanry presented a cup to be competed for in rifle shooting. It became known as the Battalion Challenge Vase. The Redditch Rifle Corps won the competition in 1888 and 1889 and as a consequence, it became the property of Captain Bartleet of Redditch.

13th Nov. 1916. BOSCO'S BUDGET. 115

JAMES COMBES.

GEO. COMBES.

EDWARD COMBES.

J. C. MOGG,
Late at Fairbank's, Bournbrook

GEO. JOHNSON.
Late B.S.A.

EUGENE JOHNSON.
Late B.S.A.

FRED JOHNSON.
Late Enfield Cycle Co.

We should feel obliged if our readers will kindly lend us Photographs of their Relatives in uniform. Postcard size preferred. Please write on the back the name and former occupation as well as the name and address to which the Photographs should be returned. We are anxious to have a complete Picture Gallery of all Redditch men who have answered their country's call.

Another page from *Bosco's Weekly* featuring more young men 'doing their bit'.

During the First World War tanks were trundled around the towns of England and used as a centre-piece for raising funds for the war effort. The tank which visited Redditch was called *Julian*.

Redditch Artillery had its headquarters on Easemore Road where they held their sports day every year. Here the gun team is going through its paces in July 1909.

The Artillery forming up in Easemore Road for military exercises in 1914.

Redditch Artillery marching down Station Approach in 1907 to board the train taking them to summer camp.

Three worthies from the Redditch Rifle Corps Volunteers. The corps was formed in 1860 and practised at the rifle range in Musketts Wood. This photograph was taken by the Redditch photographers Graham & Co. in about 1880.

Seven

Needles, Springs and Bikes

Standard Works was once part of the Allcocks fishing-tackle empire, which in the 1930s advertised itself as the biggest fishing-tackle manufacturer in the world. This photograph dates from around 1908.

Washford Mills, the home of Milwards Needles, named after the original factory which was at Washford. This photograph dates from around 1905.

Beoley paper mill, located at the bottom of Easemore Road; much of the building still exists. It was here that special acid-free paper was made to be used for wrapping needles in. This postcard was produced around 1910.

Ipsley was mentioned in the *Domesday Book* and a mill is known to have existed there at the time of William the Conqueror. The last working mill on the site was demolished in 1965. This photograph was taken about 1925.

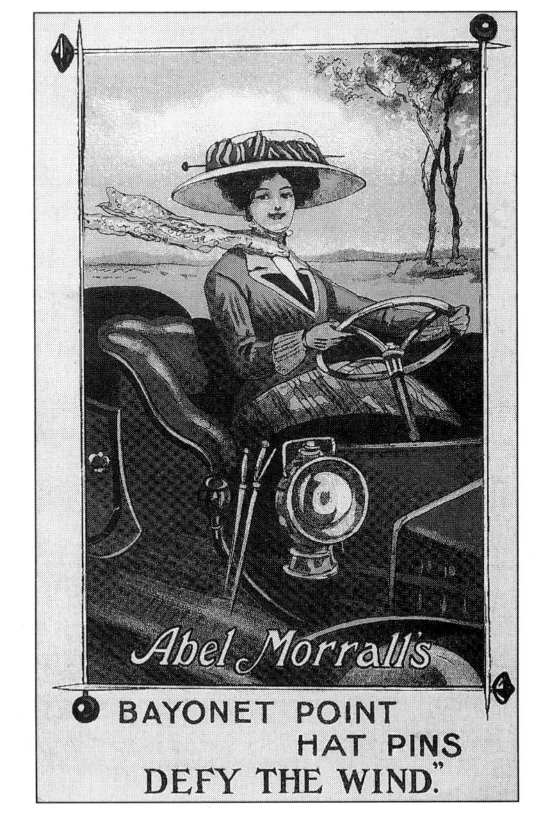

This is one of a series of postcards produced in about 1910 to advertise hat-pins. Others in the series show the same lady sailing, hot-air ballooning and motor-cycling, always using huge hat pins to secure her headgear.

A patriotic card used by Abel Morralls around the time of the First World War. The card was sent to prospective customers to announce the future visits of sales representatives.

Abel Morralls' knitting pin packing room, c. 1954. The factory stood between Edward Street and the Redditch–Birmingham railway line.

Samuel Thomas's British Mills, once the largest needle factory in the world and one of the first to be steam-powered.

Forge Mill, Redditch, which was the last working mill in Redditch when it closed in the 1950s. Saved from demolition and preserved for future generations by the efforts of dedicated enthusiasts such as the late John Rollins, it has now been converted into a needle museum.

The loading bay at Milwards Washford Mills factory, *c.* 1910.

An aerial view of the Enfield works, one of many produced at the same time, probably around the 1930s.

A brass and ceramic change dish or coaster produced between 1893 and 1897. It was obviously intended for the German market.

An original Royal Enfield Bicycle advertising postcard produced around 1910. It was used to promote the company's products and also for sales reps to send messages to customers and head office.

Enfield Road, Hunt End, *c.* 1905. The factory in the background is Royal Enfield which began manufacturing around 1892 on the site which had once belonged to Townsend Brothers.

The new Royal Enfield factory in Hewell Road before the works transferred from Hunt End. The sign behind the hedge is of C.J. Huins who built the factory. The picture was taken around the time the building work was completed.

A Royal Enfield motorcycle on a film set at Denham Studios in 1935.

A Royal Enfield 150cc Cycar. This model was introduced in the 1930s with the engine completely enclosed in a pressed steel casing. It was designed to appeal to women riders.

A Redditch Motorcycle Club outing, *c.* 1912.

Another Redditch Motorcycle Club outing, also around 1912.

Redditch Motorcycle Club's inaugural meeting at the Unicorn Hotel, Redditch in 1910. Present, from left to right: F. Hyde, T. Hyde (landlord), G. Horton, G. Mansell, H. Guise, -?-, J. Bryant, C. Hopkins, G. Davis, P. Avrill, C. Harrison, F. Viles, F. Vale, W. Skinner, E. Brough, F. Smith, R. Willis, Dr Protheroe-Smith, F. Woodfield, J. Banks, L. Sealey, J. Fisher, W. Islip, J. Davies.

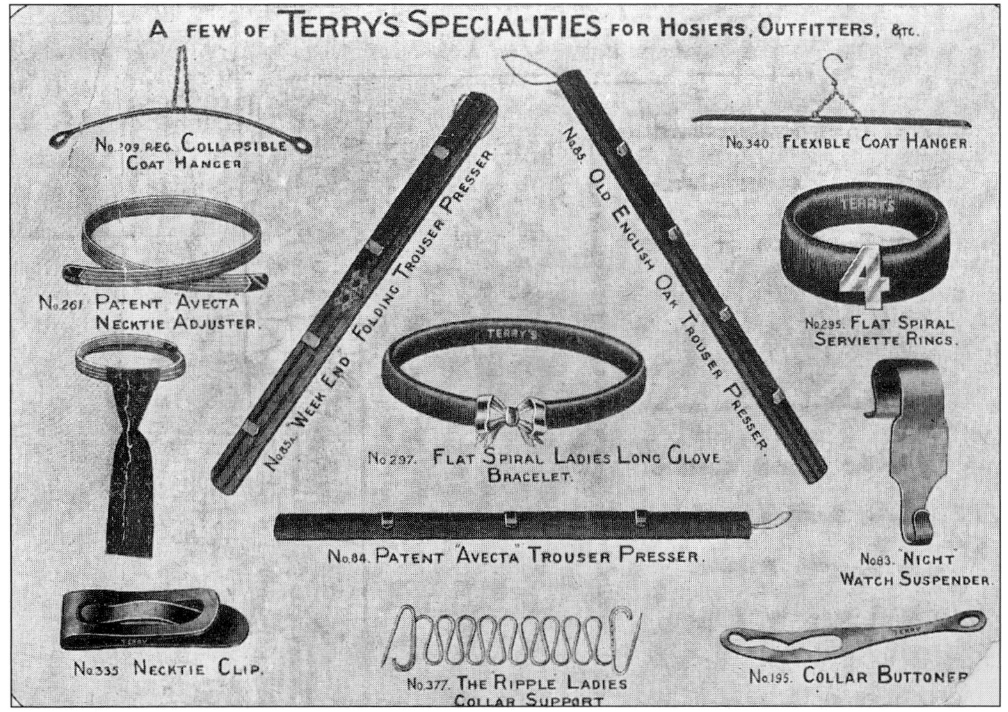

An early Terry's 'rep' card. The back is printed with the legend 'Our Mr Bayliss hopes to visit you when the favour of your esteemed orders will be much appreciated and receive careful attention.' Dating from around 1910, such cards would have been sent in advance of the salesman's visit.

A later Terry's 'rep' card with a plain back to be filled in by the sender. The card probably dates from the 1920s.

Southmead, once the home of the Milward family, overlooking their mill opposite. Eventually, it was taken over by Terry's and was finally incorporated into the canteen block. The house was demolished with the rest of the factory around 1992 to make way for the Aldi supermarket.

DON'T RISK BEING SCALDED !

Use "AVECTA"

WASHING TONGS

(Regd. No. 771872/32)

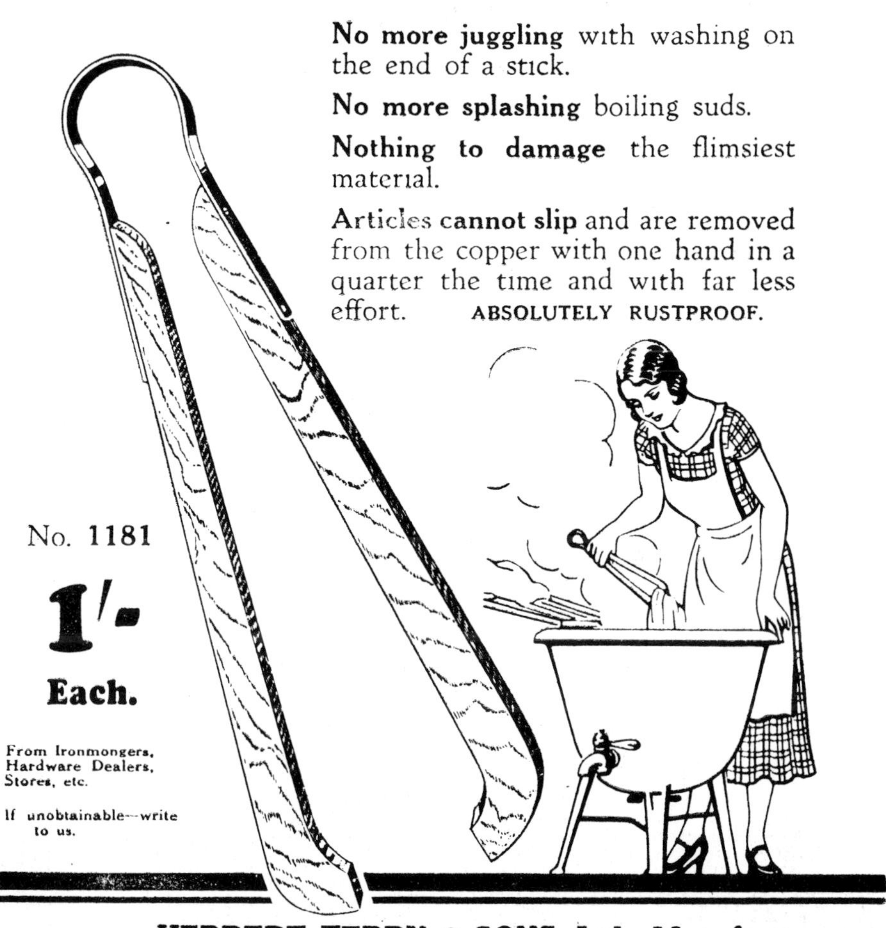

HERBERT TERRY & SONS, Ltd., Manufacturers,

REDDITCH, ENGLAND Est.1855.

London:	Birmingham:	Manchester:
27 Holborn Viaduct.	210 Corporation St.	279 Deansgate.

Terry's made hundreds of gadgets or novelties. A 1920s catalogue lists over nine hundred separate items. One of them was the washing tongs shown here and which are now becoming collector's items.

Pool Place, mis-spelt on this photograph as Poop Place! The church in the centre was incorporated into Terry's new factory building during the First World War.

Terry's stand at the BIF Exhibition at Castle Bromwich in 1937.

A Terry's dinner. Amongst those present are Norman Terry, Albert Ball, A. Victor Terry, Charles Terry and C.D. Terry.

For many years Herbert Terry's hosted a children's Christmas party in the works canteen. As well as being stuffed with jelly, cake and pop, each child also received a gift from Father Christmas. This party took place in 1949 with four hundred children attending.

Herbert Terry, the founder of the business which carried his name, was a devout Christian and a great believer in temperance which he encouraged amongst his workers. He can be seen here seated in the centre of a group photograph taken on an early outing to the Dales.

A photograph of a Terry's outing taken in the 1950s. Amongst those present are: David Coventry, Wally Powell, Audrey Coventry, Selinda Nati, Dom Nati, Mrs Powell, and Violet Aston. In the centre, at the back, is John Jakeman who managed Regent Coaches, the firm his father Harry helped to found.

A presentation dinner at Terry's in 1976. Amongst those presented with long-service awards were: Gladys Stanley, S. Thomas, G. Cund, E.V. Lamb, L. Harris, K. Clarke, G. Smith, G.H. Johnson, T.J. Hodges, Audrey Coventry, B.L. Grey, R. Lester, K.M. Tedstone, J.E. Styler, J. Hands, D. Barry and K. Earle.

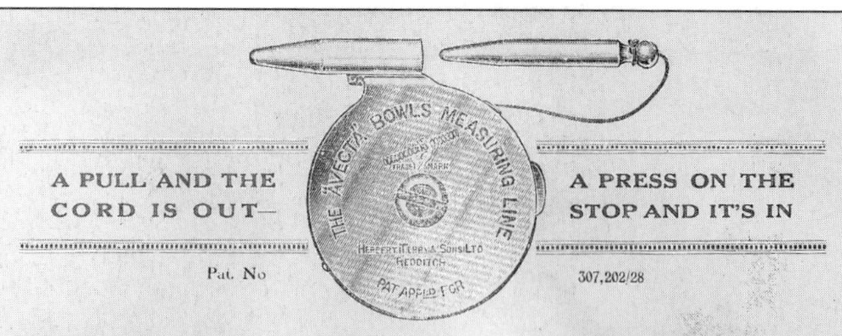

—Drake would have to measure 'em. Even when inches and empires hang in the balance—inches are very precious. Decide the inches first—finish the game—then for the Armada.

—Did Drake have difficulty in finding something to measure those tiny differences of distance between two "woods" the eye cannot gauge? How did Drake measure?

—Keenness over "shades," which decide who is, or who is not "on the jack," has not abated a bit in 300 years, yet the Bowler has been content to wind and unwind the cord off and on the pegs, with all the irritating ravelling up of the cord.

—And how many games have been decided by a straw, a piece of wood, or a match stick?

—Just fancy—for more than 300 years Bowlers have been awaiting the "TERRY" **Spring Winder** to end their difficulties in measuring.

—And here's the solution—with an audible ratchet and stop

The "AVECTA" *Bowls*
Measuring Line

—Has an aluminium case with high-class N.P. finish, which is clean to handle and hard wearing. Five feet of best quality waterproof cord is fixed to automatic spring, regulated by a micrometric ratchet and released by a thumb stop.

Weight: Less than 2-ozs. size about 2 inches diameter.

Price **4/-** *each.*

:: :: From Sports Dealers, Ironmongers, or in case of difficulty, from us.

A handbill advertising a Herbert Terry bowls measure from the 1920s.